Benedict
CUMBER**STITCH**

Benedict CUMBERSTITCH

CROSS STITCH MR CUMBERBATCH IN 15 GREAT PATTERNS

Colleen Carrington

Photography by Rita Platts

KYLE BOOKS

To Richard, my real-life leading man.

First published in Great Britain in 2015 by
Kyle Books, an imprint of Kyle Cathie Ltd
192–198 Vauxhall Bridge Road
London SW1V 1DX
general.enquiries@kylebooks.com
www.kylebooks.com

10 9 8 7 6 5 4 3 2 1

ISBN 978 0 85783 324 2

Project Editor: Tara O'Sullivan
Photographer: Rita Platts
Illustrator: Kuo Kang Chen
Prop Stylist: Wei Tang
Production: Lisa Pinnell

A Cataloguing in Publication record for this title is available from the British Library.

Colour reproduction by Alta London
Printed and bound in China by C&C Offset Printing Co., Ltd.

Contents

Welcome to Benedict Cumber**stitch!**

Within this book you will find 15 cross stitch patterns inspired by the career and charisma of the actor Benedict Cumberbatch. The patterns are of varying difficulty but all follow the same easy principles of cross stitch.

Getting started

Most cross stitch is worked on fabric which looks like a grid, called Aida. Look to the pattern to see how big a piece is required to stitch the design. Be sure to cut extra fabric all around to make for easy framing.

The pattern will also tell you which count of Aida you need. The count of the fabric refers to how many stitches per inch it will hold. A higher count fabric will make the finished design smaller. You can hold Aida in your hand to stitch on, but for bigger pieces you may find a hoop makes things easier.

The designs in this book are all worked with DMC stranded cotton. Refer to the colour numbers in the pattern key. If you prefer to use a different brand, conversion charts are readily available online. The key will also tell you how many strands to make each stitch with. Stranded cotton is made up of 6 strands — separate out how many you need at a time.

YOU WILL NEED

- **cross stitch fabric**
- **stranded cotton thread**
- **size 24 or 26 tapestry needles**
- **a small pair of scissors**

Always stitch with clean hands and pack your cross stitch away when not working on it.

Stitching

Locate the middle of your fabric. It will be easier to start here as the exact centre of the design is marked on the chart with black arrows. Fold your fabric in half one way and then the other and lightly crease it near the centre to mark a faint cross. If you want to start somewhere else, count the number of squares from the middle to your chosen starting point on the chart and find the same point on on your fabric by counting out from the middle. Load your needle with the required number of strands in the correct colour. The thread's length should reach no further than your elbow when you hold your needle in your hand to stitch.

Each square on the grid on the chart makes one cross stitch on your fabric. Every square on the fabric has a hole in each corner to stitch through. You make a cross stitch by stitching a cross with two diagonal stitches, as shown below.

You can stitch in rows (doing one set of diagonal lines followed by the other) or by doing each cross stitch at a time. Always make the first stitch of the crosses go in the same direction; your finished work will look much neater if you do this.

Following the pattern, build up the picture by stitching blocks of colour at a time. Pull the thread through tightly enough that it lies flat on the fabric but not so tightly that it distorts the holes.

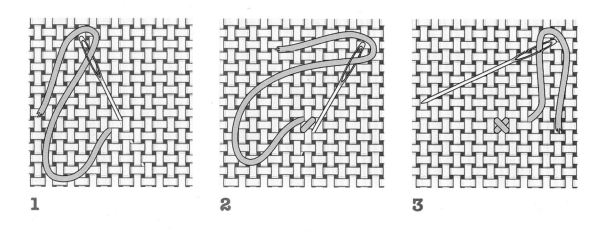

1   2   3

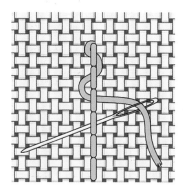

Trapping You have to trap the start and end of your thread underneath the stitches you make on the reverse side. Hold it in place with a finger when you start and simply run it under stitches to finish. Snip off any remaining thread close to the surface.

Do you find your thread becomes tangled or your stitches aren't lying flat? Try using shorter lengths of thread and keep the 'tail' of the thread long as it comes through the needle.

Backstitch

Some patterns require this stitch to finish them or as part of the main design. Backstitch is indicated by the black or coloured bold lines. Use the holes in the fabric to make your stitches just like with cross stitch. Check the notes to see how many strands are required. Make your stitch every time the line on the pattern goes over a hole. Start and end by trapping your thread under existing stitches. Sometimes you need to trap the starting end underneath backstitches you make.

Stitch backstitch on top of the cross stitches. See how you always come 'back' on yourself?

1

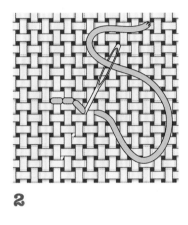
2

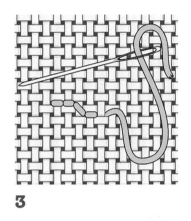
3

Other techniques and tips

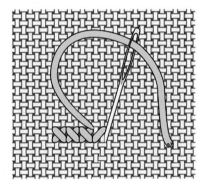

Evenweave Some designs are worked on 'evenweave' fabric. This is a finer fabric with twice the amount of holes per inch for the fabric count. For example, 32 count evenweave is treated as 16 count fabric. You stitch over two holes at a time instead of one to make your cross stitches.

You will need to hold evenweave fabric in a hoop or frame as it is not stiff like Aida.

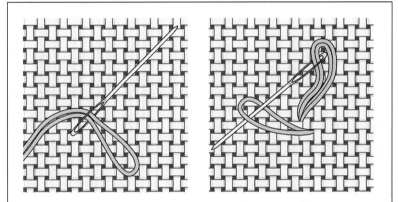

Doubled over thread If you're having trouble starting, try using one strand of thread in your needle doubled over to make two. This leaves a loop at one end of your thread that you can use to secure it on the reverse side as you make the first half of a cross stitch.

Finishing off

Your completed work can be safely ironed face down on an ironing board using a hot heat setting with plenty of steam. It can also be washed in warm water with dish soap if required. You can then mount the fabric onto board ready for framing. Use a background the same colour as the fabric.

That's everything – you're ready to get started!

Sherlock

Cumberbatch's best known and loved role, now in cross stitch form.

Benedict, I deduce you have the best cheekbones in the business.

★

DESIGN 100 x 103 stitches

STITCHED ON 18 count white Aida

USE 2 strands of thread

FINISHED SIZE 14.11 x 14.53cm / 5.56 x 5.72 inches

★

Benedict hates Sherlock's hair. In an interview with Caitlin Moran for *The Times Magazine*, he said: 'I can't think of a wittier or even more accurate comparison, but I just think it makes me look a bit like…a woman.' Well, Benedict, we think you look great!

Good cross stitch technique means that the back of your project should look almost as neat as the front. Here is an example of how the back of a well-stitched project looks.

KEY for SHERLOCK

SYMBOL	DMC	COLOUR NAME	SYMBOL	DMC	COLOUR NAME
■	310	black	✕	3799	anthracite grey
▼	317	steel grey	Γ	414	granite grey
◣	938	espresso brown	◆	758	pale terracotta
◖	948	pale peach	⊙	951	winter white
◪	336	indigo blue	✚	336	night blue
—	322	delft blue			

Simple **portrait**

With this design you can stitch a Benedict for any setting or occasion. Why not have his charming smile adorn your desk at the office or brighten up your bedroom? This is a simple project, perfect for beginners. Stitch his central features first. At the end of each area, tuck and trim your thread off before moving onto new areas rather than trail your thread across the back. This will give a neater finish.

★

DESIGN **51 x 77 stitches**

STITCHED ON **14 count white Aida**

USE **2 strands of thread**

FINISHED SIZE **9.3 x 14cm / 3.6 x 5.5 inches**

★

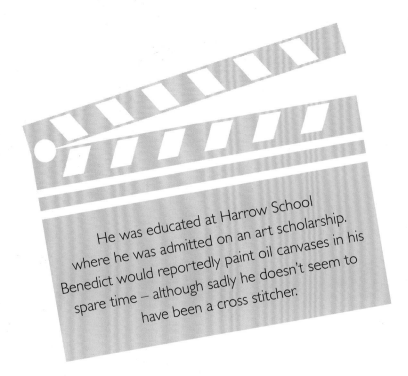

He was educated at Harrow School where he was admitted on an art scholarship. Benedict would reportedly paint oil canvases in his spare time – although sadly he doesn't seem to have been a cross stitcher.

16

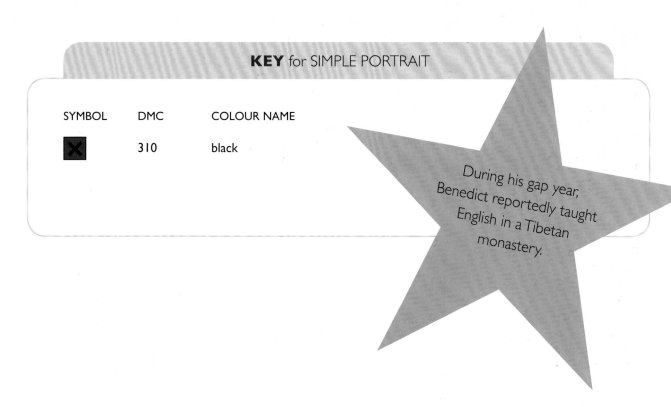

SYMBOL	DMC	COLOUR NAME
✖	310	black

During his gap year, Benedict reportedly taught English in a Tibetan monastery.

TIP: framing your project

After your work has been ironed, it will be ready to be framed. You could simply display your cross stitch within a hoop. Gather up the Aida round the edges and use spare thread to fix it out of the way at the back.

For a frame, you need to mount the cross stitch onto stiff board using a technique called 'lacing' to fit the frame. Choose acid-free board so that the fabric doesn't discolour. Position your work on the board and turn it face down. Fold the edges of the Aida over the board and use strong thread to 'lace' opposite edges of Aida together across the board, the tighter the better. Observe the tension of the Aida from the front and adjust your lacing so that the Aida lays flat all over. It is then ready for the frame.

For evenweave fabric or large projects, you may prefer the results from a framer, who will stretch and lace your work professionally.

There are lots of creative ways to display cross stitch. As it is a fibre art, you could make a cross stitch design into a cushion, or even stitch onto a bag or shirt using waste canvas.

On the **Red** Carpet

Here is that instantly recognisable silhouette as he poses for snaps on the red carpet at a glittering event. This is a simple design that uses blocks of bold colour to create the image without including detail. If you'd rather be stitching those famous facial features, try the Simple Portrait on page 14 - or, if you're up for more of a challenge, the Detailed Portrait on page 60.

★

DESIGN **63 x 116** stitches

STITCHED ON **14 count white Aida**

USE **2 strands of thread**

FINISHED SIZE **11.4 x 21.1cm / 4.5 x 8.3 inches**

★

BENEDICT CUMBER**STITCH**

SYMBOL	DMC	COLOUR NAME	SYMBOL	DMC	COLOUR NAME
■	310	black	◆	3799	anthracite grey
✕	606	red orange	▽	726	mimosa yellow

His full name is
Benedict Timothy Carlton Cumberbatch
and he was born on 19th July 1976.

BENEDICT CUMBER**STITCH**

x x x x x x x x x x x x x x x x x x x x x x x x x x x x x x x x x x x x x x x x x x x x x x x x x x x

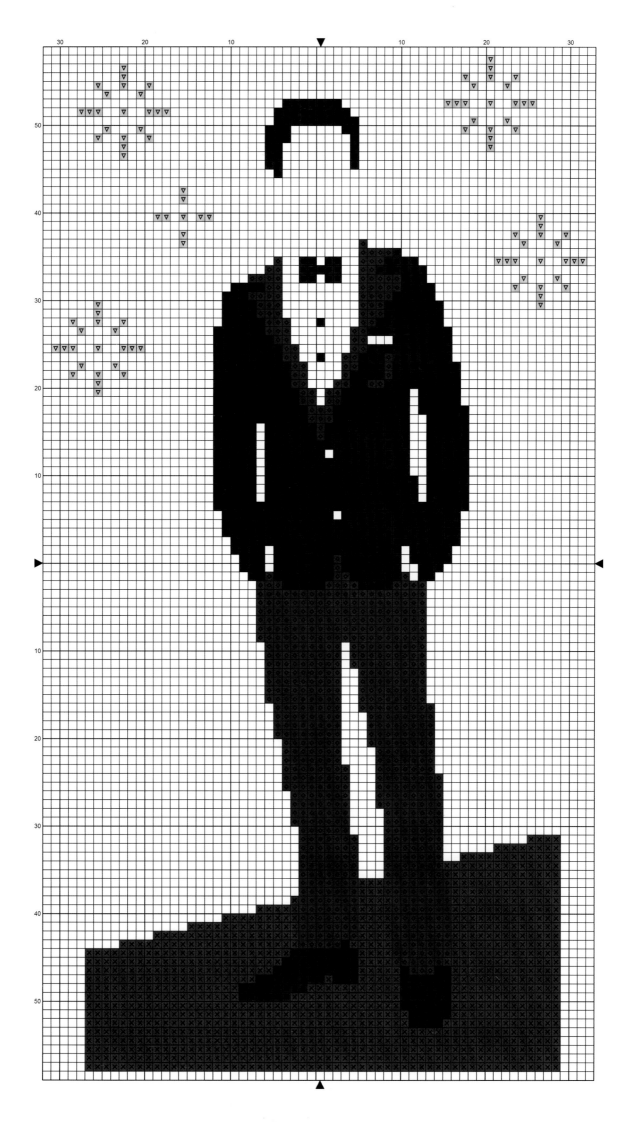

Otter or **Cumberbatch?**

Here he is looking rather dapper and smart in his best get-up, perhaps on his way to a glitzy premier. Benedict doesn't look bad either. For any Cumberbatch fans who missed the internet trend for finding photographs of otters that look like Benedict – you kinda had to be there.

★

DESIGN **83 x 50** stitches

STITCHED ON **16** count white Aida

USE **2** strands of thread

FINISHED SIZE **13.2 x 7.9cm / 5.2 x 3.1** inches

★

KEY for OTTER OR CUMBERBATCH

SYMBOL	DMC	COLOUR NAME
■	310	black
▽	317	steel grey
■	300	mahogany
∩	842	beige rope
◆	758	dawn rose
↑	3755	pastel blue
✕	3799	anthracite grey
⊙	3865	winter white
✚	840	hare brown
−	543	shell beige
⦓	951	light eggshell cream

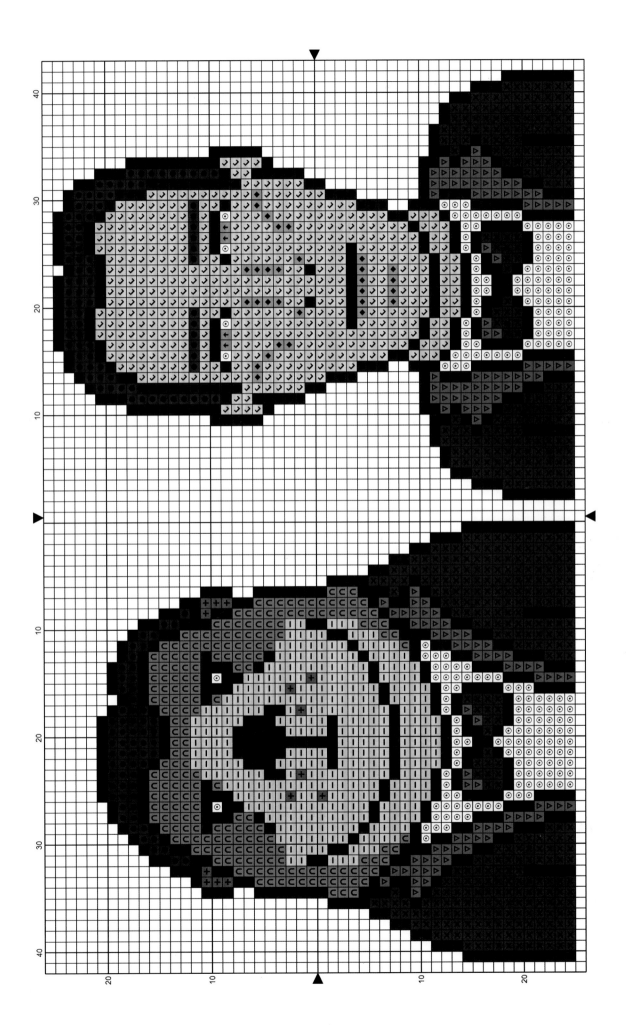

Dragonbatch

Oh Benedict, you did make some funny faces when acting the fearsome dragon. Here you can have the wings you worked so hard to emulate.

★

DESIGN **88 x 56 stitches**

STITCHED ON **14 count white Aida**

USE **2 strands of thread**

FINISHED SIZE **16 x 10.2cm / 6.3 x 4 inches**

★

KEY for DRAGONBATCH

SYMBOL	DMC	COLOUR NAME
■	310	black
✖	721	papaya orange
◤	300	mahogany
◣	407	clay brown
▬	3755	pastel blue
◆	900	saffron orange
▽	722	orange spice
⅀	301	squirrel brown
✚	951	light eggshell cream
⊙	3865	winter white

Oscarbatch

And the award goes to... OK, so at the time of writing, Benedict's yet to win an Oscar, but we all know he deserves one. While we wait for the announcement, stitch this statuette version of the man himself in golden tones in honour of his fabulous acting career.

DESIGN **75 x 140 stitches**

STITCHED ON **16 count white Aida**

USE **2 strands of thread**

FINISHED SIZE **11.9 x 22.2cm / 4.7 x 8.8 inches**

While filming *To The Ends of the Earth* in KwaZulu-Natal, South Africa, in 2005, Benedict and his companions were reportedly kidnapped by armed robbers before being released in the middle of nowhere.

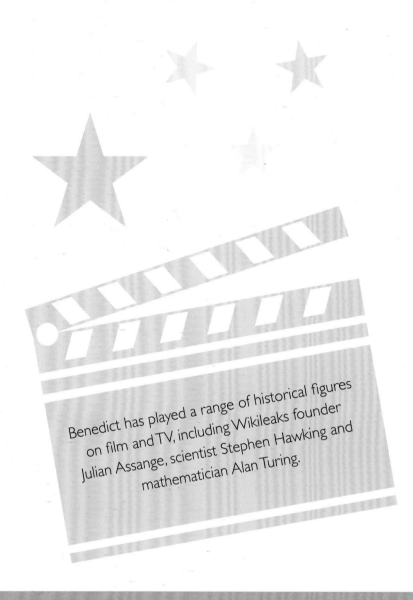

Benedict has played a range of historical figures on film and TV, including Wikileaks founder Julian Assange, scientist Stephen Hawking and mathematician Alan Turing.

KEY for OSCARBATCH

SYMBOL	DMC	COLOUR NAME	SYMBOL	DMC	COLOUR NAME
■	310	black	●	3799	anthracite grey
◈	413	iron grey	◣	414	lead grey
◆	3852	mustard yellow	✕	3820	maize yellow
▽	3821	straw yellow	⊥	3822	light straw yellow
▬	666	bright red	⊙	3865	winter white

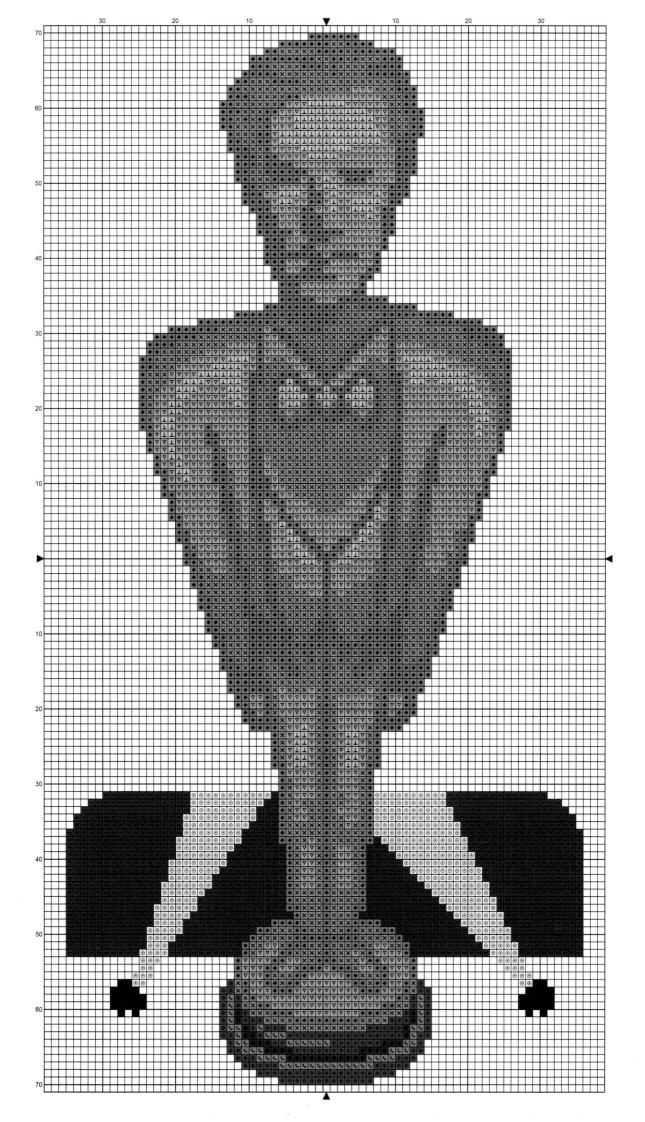

Frankenstein

During the run of this National Theatre production, Benedict shared the
roles of both creator and monster with Jonny Lee Miller.

★

DESIGN 167 x 118 stitches

STITCHED ON 18 count white Aida

USE 2 strands of thread for cross stitch

USE 1 strand of thread for backstitch

FINISHED SIZE 23.6 x 16.7cm / 9.3 x 6.6 inches

★

KEY for FRANKENSTEIN

SYMBOL	DMC	COLOUR NAME
■	310	black
Z	3799	anthracite grey
∪	317	steel grey
⌐	648	pepper grey
↑	930	slate grey
·	762	pearl grey
0	842	beige rope
9	948	pale peach
⊙	3865	winter white
3	976	nutmeg brown
◇	844	pepper black
+	413	iron grey
−	646	platinum grey
U	3072	pale pearl grey
T	931	blue grey
≋	407	clay brown
X	3779	pale terracotta
Ɛ	ecru	ecru
▣	301	squirrel brown
6	3705	pale red
▭	648	pepper grey

Work the cross stitches before the backstitch detail

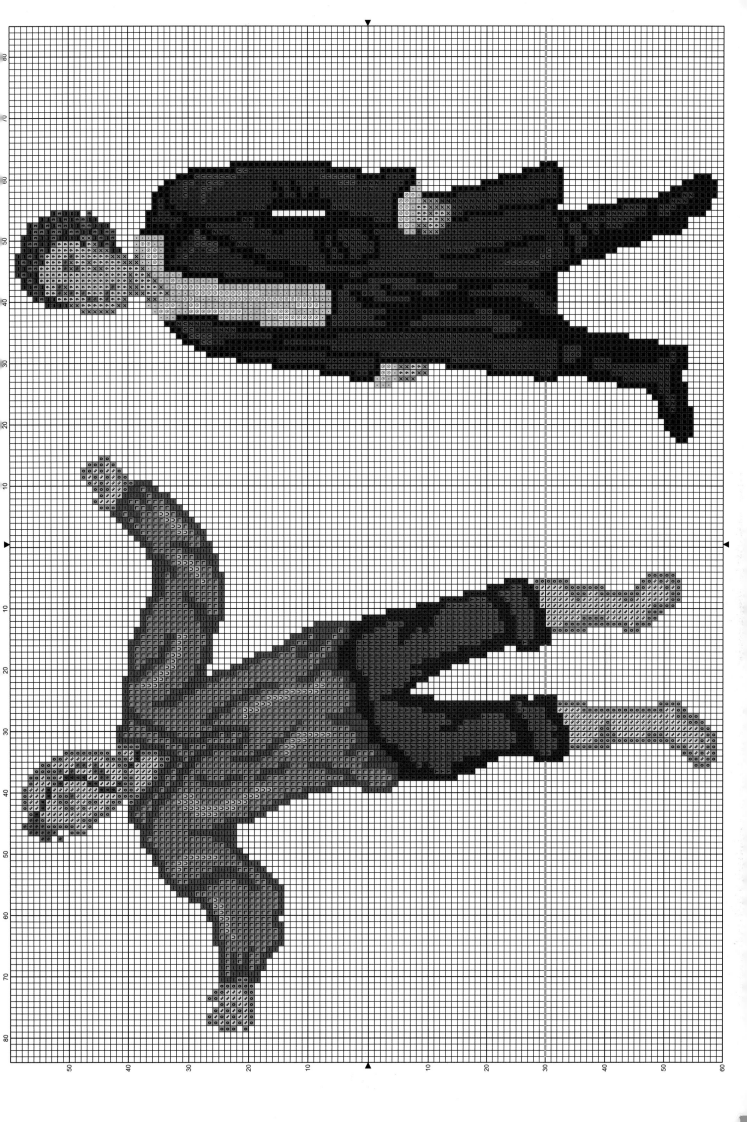

Hamlet

The intense gaze says it all. Benedict delivers his soliloquy as Hamlet.

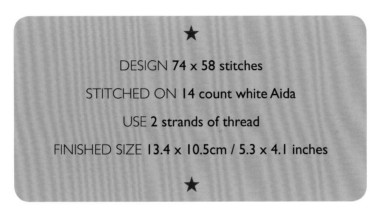

★

DESIGN **74 x 58 stitches**

STITCHED ON **14 count white Aida**

USE **2 strands of thread**

FINISHED SIZE **13.4 x 10.5cm / 5.3 x 4.1 inches**

★

According to IMDb, one of Benedict's first acting roles was playing Titania, the Queen of Fairies, in Shakespeare's *A Midsummer Night's Dream* at Harrow when he was thirteen.

In March 2014, Cumberbatch was included in the *Sunday Times* '100 Makers of the 21st Century' list, which cited him as the 'next Sir Laurence Olivier'.

KEY for HAMLET

SYMBOL	DMC	COLOUR NAME	SYMBOL	DMC	COLOUR NAME
✖	413	iron grey	▽	415	chrome grey
⊙	3865	winter white	◣	758	dawn rose
◈	951	light eggshell cream	■	300	mahogany
✚	301	squirrel brown	◤	910	dark emerald green
▬	3755	pastel blue			

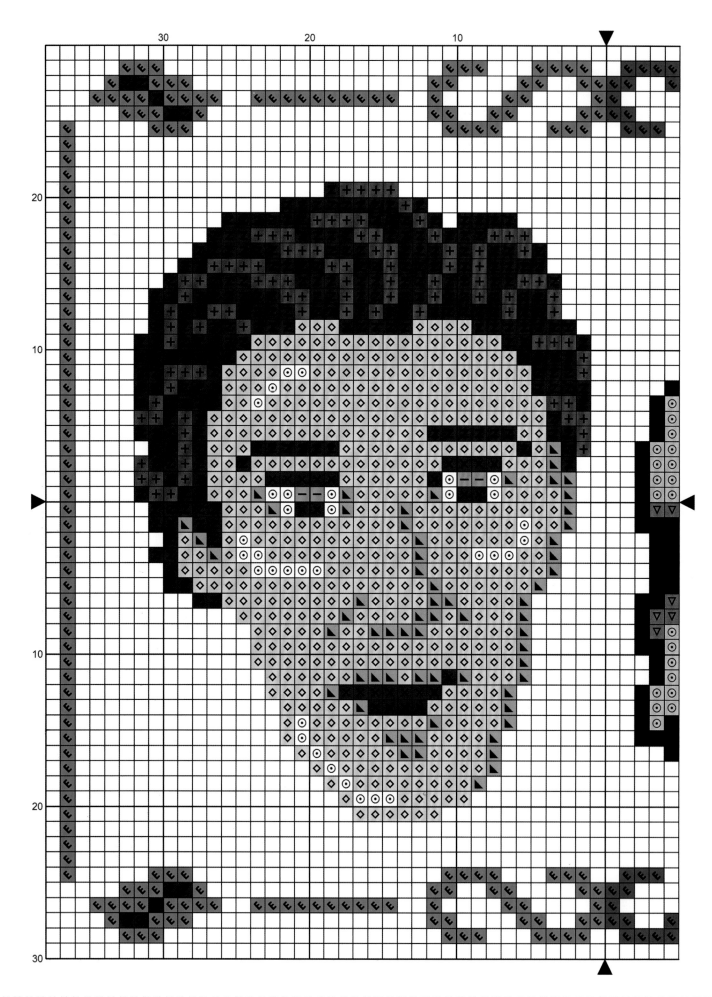

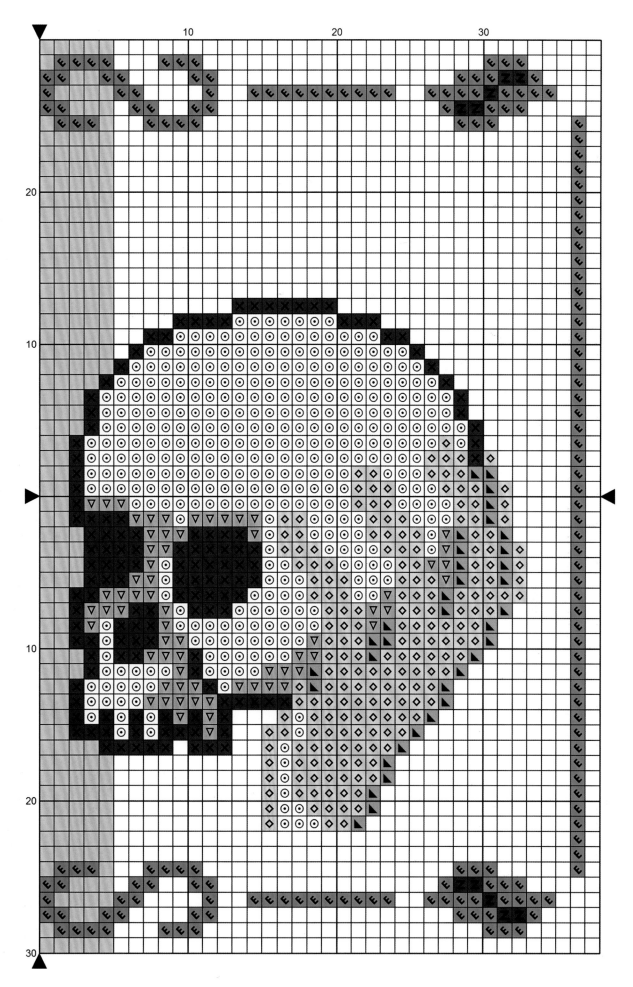

Sampler

No cross stitch collection would be complete without a sampler. Celebrating Benedict's roles and personality, the design includes his Britannia Award (British Artist of the Year 2013) and Emmy Statuette (Outstanding Lead Actor for *Sherlock*, 2014).

★

DESIGN 153 x 107 stitches

STITCHED ON 18 count white Aida

USE 2 strands of thread

FINISHED SIZE 21.6 x 15.1cm / 8.5 x 6 inches

★

KEY for SAMPLER

SYMBOL	DMC	COLOUR NAME	SYMBOL	DMC	COLOUR NAME
✖	666	bright red	U	3705	pale red
❮	3326	wild rose	◆	798	cobalt blue
▽	3755	pastel blue	⊥	775	summer rain blue

benedict
cumberbatch

Photobomb

Look out celebs! No award ceremony will be safe again thanks to
Mr Cumberbatch and his hilarious photobombing antics. Consider using your
own custom colours to personalise the photobomb-ees in the design.

★

DESIGN **57 x 110 stitches**

STITCHED ON **16 count white Aida**

USE **2 strands of thread for cross stitch**

USE **1 strand of thread 310 for backstitch**

USE **2 strands of thread 928 as longstitch for detail on phone screen**

FINISHED SIZE **9 x 17.5cm / 3.6 x 6.9 inches**

★

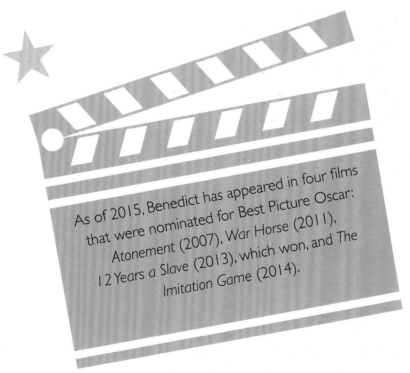

As of 2015, Benedict has appeared in four films
that were nominated for Best Picture Oscar:
Atonement (2007), War Horse (2011),
12 Years a Slave (2013), which won, and The
Imitation Game (2014).

TIP: how to do longstitch

This design requires you to stitch the menu functions on the phone screen using two strands of thread 928. The technique you'll need to use for this is called 'longstitch' which is a variation of backstitch. Stitch the phone menu details using long single stitches rather than going across each hole in the fabric like in basic backstitch. This creates a bolder look for the pale thread on a dark background.

Long-stitches tend to be looser than normal backstitch. Carefully trap the start of your thread by running it underneath existing stitches on the reverse side as normal. Consider running it under more than you would for normal backstitch. Finish off in the same way and snip the thread close to the surface.

KEY for PHOTOBOMB

SYMBOL	DMC	COLOUR NAME	SYMBOL	DMC	COLOUR NAME
■	310	black	Z	3799	anthracite grey
∩	317	steel grey	Γ	647	rock grey
✚	648	pepper grey	↑	3756	cloud blue
⊙	3865	winter white	◆	754	beige rose
✗	948	pale peach	▽	3705	pale red
◈	434	cigar brown	◿	3863	otter brown
Є	612	string brown	◖	613	rope brown
─	834	light brass	⋋	932	seagull blue
•	996	electric blue	⊘	3761	light sky blue
6	3042	lilac	T	3743	pale lilac
9	966	baby green	★	743	medium yellow
──	310	black backstitch	──	928	light pearl grey longstitch

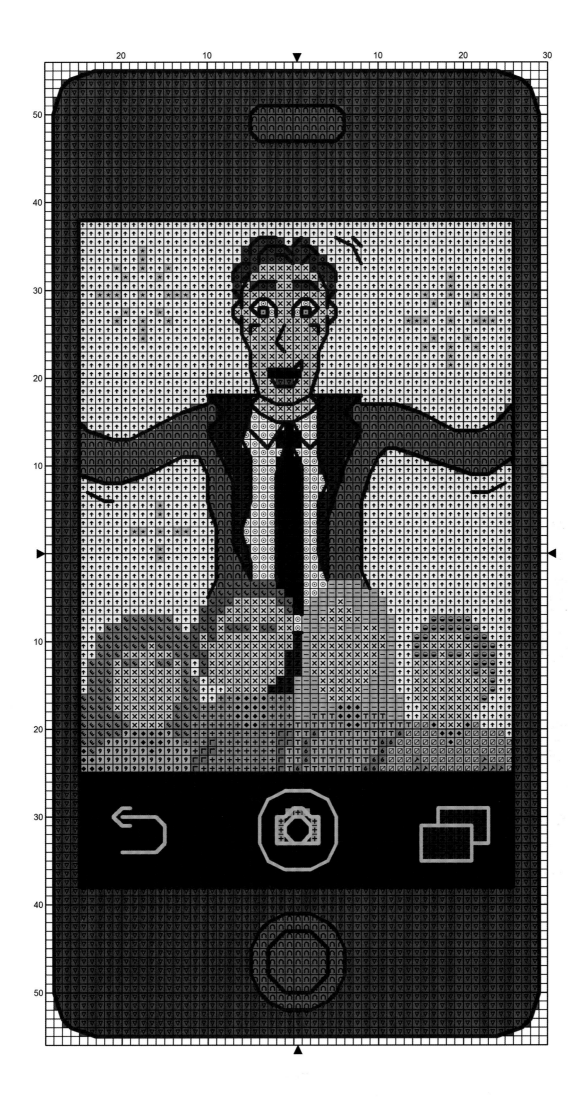

Classic Holmes

A salute to the super-sleuth circa 1895.

★

DESIGN **71 x 95** stitches

STITCHED ON **16** count white Aida

USE **2** strands of thread

FINISHED SIZE **11.27 x 15.08** cm / **4.44 x 5.94** inches

★

BENEDICT CUMBER**STITCH**

44

KEY for CLASSIC HOLMES

SYMBOL	DMC	COLOUR NAME	SYMBOL	DMC	COLOUR NAME
■	310	black	▼	3781	metal brown
✕	611	sisal brown	∩	612	string brown
◤	613	rope brown	◆	407	clay brown
◤	3779	pale terracotta	—	948	pale peach
┌	739	dune cream	o	712	cream
■	3857	dark red wine	+	3858	medium red wine
T	919	red copper	Ɛ	921	burnt ochre orange

Benedict's voice can be heard on a number of audio books, voicing, among other things, Shakespeare works and Sherlock Holmes novels. He has also voiced radio programmes including the popular comedy Cabin Pressure and the war-time drama My Dear Bessie.

Dancing with Fassbender

Recreate in stitches the glorious moment Benedict threw some shapes with Michael Fassbender at the 2014 Golden Globes.

★

DESIGN 102 x 76 stitches

STITCHED ON 16 count black Aida

USE 2 strands of thread

FINISHED SIZE 16.19 x 12.06 cm / 6.38 x 4.75 inches

★

It can be tricky stitching dark colours on black fabric. Rather than use a direct light source, stitch in natural light. Place something white on your lap like a tea-towel or spare piece of Aida. This will provide a contrast and make the holes in your fabric easier to see as you stitch. Try the design on any bright coloured Aida. If you use a lower count fabric than 16, stitch using 3 strands for optimum coverage and to stop the colour of the fabric showing through.

KEY for DANCING WITH FASSBENDER

SYMBOL	DMC	COLOUR NAME	SYMBOL	DMC	COLOUR NAME
■	310	black	◆	3799	anthracite grey
✖	317	steel grey	▽	3756	cloud blue
◆	407	clay brown	U	3779	pale terracotta
✚	948	pale peach	Z	801	mink brown
◼	433	chocolate brown	⧄	434	cigar brown
⊥	3045	coffee cream	◄	436	teddy brown
F	3776	dark nutmeg brown			

50

Richard III

Capture Benedict's brooding acting intensity in cross stitch as the infamous king. Benedict is actually Richard III's second cousin, 16 times removed.

★

DESIGN **89 x 89 stitches**

STITCHED ON **16 count white Aida**

USE **2 strands of thread**

FINISHED SIZE **14.1 x 14.1cm / 5.6 x 5.6 inches**

★

TIP: how to care for your materials

I like to store all my fabric in grip-seal bags inside plastic containers to keep out dust and pet hair from my very fluffy cat. This is the same for any cross stitch project I'm working on. If a project or sewing bits travel with me, they stay in their grip-seal organisers within my sewing bag.

Does it ever seem that your needle starts to feel grubby? The oils in your fingers react with the metal causing it to tarnish. You may notice a dark mark appear on your needle where you hold it most. Change your needle when this happens, as it can mark your fabric. For the serious stitcher, consider using gold- or platinum-plated needles and they'll last until they're snapped or lost!

I keep my thread wound onto bobbins and stored in plastic sewing boxes. Each bobbin is marked with the corresponding DMC colour number and stored numerically. That way, I can easily pick out colours needed for any pattern that calls for a particular number. DMC thread colour descriptions may vary from country to country, but the colour numbers are the same all over the world.

KEY for RICHARD III

SYMBOL	DMC	COLOUR NAME	SYMBOL	DMC	COLOUR NAME
■	310	black	◆	3799	anthracite grey
∩	413	iron grey	✕	317	steel grey
Z	414	lead grey	⊥	318	granite grey
—	415	chrome grey	▽	801	mink brown
◆	407	clay brown	◁	950	beige
A	3852	mustard yellow	O	3821	straw yellow
♥	816	red fruit	E	910	dark emerald green

Eyes

Capture Benedict's most colourful feature with a few cross stitches and some simple line detailing in backstitch.

DESIGN **115 x 30 stitches**

STITCHED ON **32 count evenweave (Murano in ivory)**

USE **2 strands of thread for cross stitch**

USE **2 strands to backstitch in 823 around the iris**

USE **1 strand of 310 for all other backstitch**

FINISHED SIZE **18.3 x 4.8cm / 7.2 x 1.9 inches**

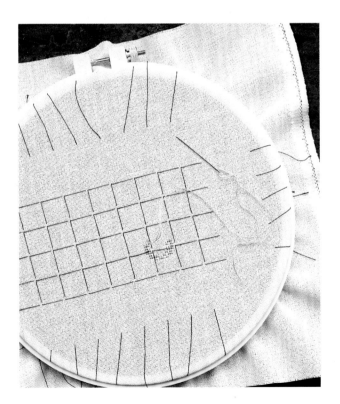

Use a hoop when stitching on evenweave. To help you find your place to start and to ease counting over empty areas, try 'gridding' your fabric before you start.

Make a grid on your fabric to match the major grid lines on the chart. Use thread that can be easily pulled out later such as single strand polyester thread or even fishing wire. Mark out blocks of ten squares using a running stitch as shown.

Stitch all the cross stitches first. Backstitch the blue around the iris before the rest of the backstitch detailing. Carefully trap the ends of your backstitching thread under the stitches you make. You can gently pull out your grid lines at any stage. If preferred, you can stitch on 16 or 18 count Aida.

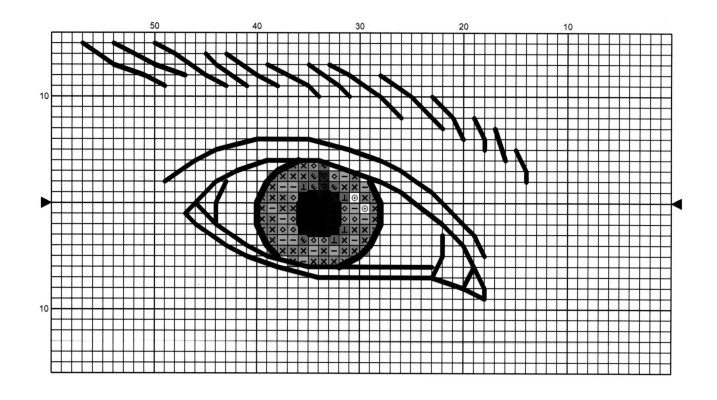

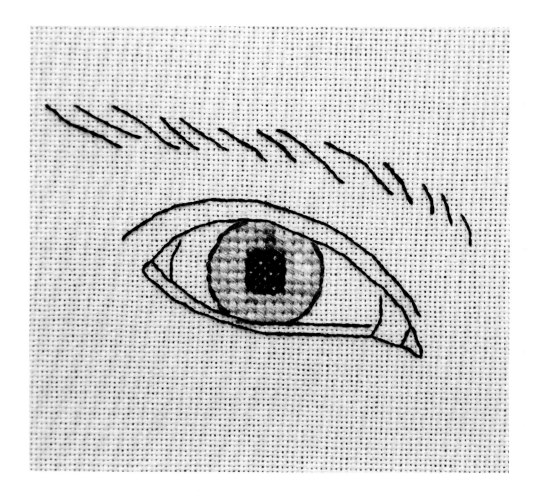

BENEDICT CUMBER**STITCH**

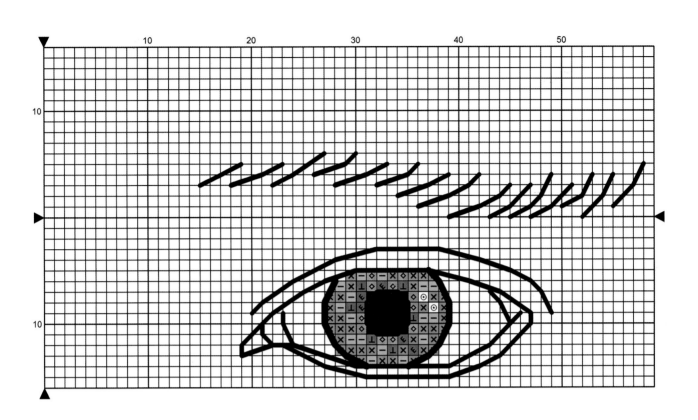

KEY for EYES

SYMBOL	DMC	COLOUR NAME
■	310	black
▬	598	lagoon turquoise
Ɛ	680	dark old gold
◈	3013	resin green
✕	597	Iceland blue
◤	400	brown
⊥	371	green plains
⊙	3865	winter white
—	310	black
—	823	blueberry blue

According to IMDb, Benedict has a condition called heterochromia, which is why he has different colours in his eyes.

Detailed Portrait

Create a contemporary portrait of Benedict in a timeless greyscale for a work you'll want to hang in pride of place.

DESIGN 113 x 153 stitches

STITCHED ON **32 count Belfast linen (antique white)**

USE **2 strands of thread for cross stitch**

USE **1 strand for all backstitch**

FINISHED SIZE **17.9 x 24.3cm / 7.1 x 9.6 inches**

This project is stitched on 32 count antique white evenweave Belfast linen. If preferred you can stitch on 16 or 18 count Aida.

Stitch all the cross stitches first, then backstitch around the iris using 1 strand of 413. Stitch this before the rest of the backstitch using 1 strand of 310.

When backstitch is used in a repeated pattern, as it is here, it is called 'blackwork'.

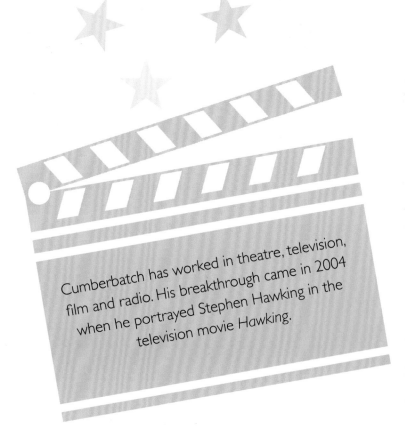

Cumberbatch has worked in theatre, television, film and radio. His breakthrough came in 2004 when he portrayed Stephen Hawking in the television movie Hawking.

BENEDICT CUMBER**STITCH**

x x x x x x x x x x x x x x x x x x x x x x x x x x x x x x x x x x x x x x x x x x x x x x x x x x x x x x x x x x x x x x x x x x x x x x x x

60

KEY for DETAILED PORTRAIT

SYMBOL	DMC	COLOUR NAME	SYMBOL	DMC	COLOUR NAME
■	310	black	✖	413	iron grey
Z	414	lead grey	U	318	granite grey
T	415	chrome grey	–	762	pearl grey
⊙	3865	winter white	▬	310	black
			▭	413	iron grey

TIP: working on a detailed project

Cross stitch follows the same basic principles but refined technique comes with practice. I suggest you stitch a detailed design like this portrait when you are confident in your technique. It is important to keep the same thread tension throughout the project for the best result. You'll see that there are larger areas of one colour as well as areas with lots of colour changes. The more uniform these look when stitched, the more photo-real your work will look. A hoop or sewing frame with help you with this. Make sure you are comfortable, have lots of natural light and don't rush to finish your stitching.

Always make your cross stitches in the same direction and take extra care to trap the ends of your thread as they will be more easily seen through the finer evenweave fabric. If you feel daunted during your project have a break and move onto something smaller and easier. If you make a mistake, find it and undo stitches to re-stitch correctly rather than fudge it over. The satisfaction of a job well done will be worth it in the end.

Acknowledgements

I would like to thank my Project Editor Tara O'Sullivan for the fabulous original idea that is *Benedict Cumberstitch*, and for all her guidance, wisdom and patience in turning this idea into my first published work.

Thank you to Rita Platts for your stunning and dynamic photography. I never dreamed my cross stitch could look this good! My thanks also to Rita's assistant Joanna Flaczynska for all her skill and hard work, to Wei Tang for the inspired styling, and to the designer Isobel Gillan for bringing my patterns to life with your gorgeous design.

And thank you Benedict Cumberbatch x